I don't have all the a
I don't always know w....... ....
But I'm no longer afraid of not knowing.
Because I trust what's unfolding inside of me.
I trust the soft voice that says, "Keep going."
Even when I don't recognize myself — especially then —
I remind myself: This is the becoming.

It's not polished.
It's not perfect.
But it's honest.
It's raw.
It's real.

There are days I bloom, and days I break.
But every version of me is sacred.
Even the one that's unsure.
Even the one that still cries at night.

-Keesh

 444™: For Better, For Worse, Forever Becoming

Table of Contents

Forever Becoming

"I used to think 'becoming' had a finish line... but becoming doesn't look like arriving; it's evolving."

Forever Believing

"Belief isn't always loud — sometimes it's whispering 'maybe' while your whole world screams 'no.'"

Forever Growing

"Growth doesn't always come from healing. Sometimes it comes from heartbreak, betrayal and loss."

Forever Chosen

"There's a heartbreak that doesn't come from lovers, but from the people who were supposed to choose you."

 444™: For Better, For Worse, Forever Becoming

Forever Healing

"Healing isn't soft music and bubble baths — it's messy, lonely, exhausting... but necessary."

Forever Grace

"Before I could become who I'm meant to be, I had to forgive myself — grace doesn't excuse, it frees."

Forever Love

"If it doesn't feel safe, if it demands you shrink or silence your soul — it's not love."

 444™: For Better, For Worse, Forever Becoming

Chapter One: Forever Becoming

I used to think "becoming" had a finish line.
That one day I'd wake up healed, whole, and untouched by what hurt me.
But the truth is... becoming doesn't look like arriving.
It looks like evolving. Over and over again.
It's learning how to grieve who you were while reaching for who you're called to be.

Some days I'm so proud of how far I've come.
Other days I mourn the girl who kept quiet just to survive.
But I've made peace with both —
Because both of them lived inside me for a reason.

Now, I'm giving myself permission to change,
To grow,
To outgrow,
To try again — even when the world says "you should've healed by now."

I'm no longer rushing my process.
I'm honoring it.
And even when it's messy — I still deserve love, grace, and softness.

I am... Forever. Becoming.

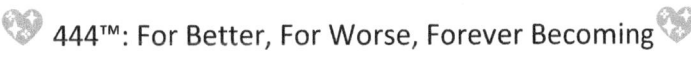

The Becoming Declaration

I was told I'd never amount to much.
They tried to break me at a young age.
Tried to dim my light before I even understood the power
of my glow.

But there was always something inside me —
a flicker,
a whisper,
a flame —
that refused to go out.

Even at this moment...
I've probably only used 2% of my potential.
And still — look at how I shine. WHEW!!!
Look at how I rise.

In this lifetime, I know what my assignment is.
Love.
To grow it. Nurture it.
And give it away like bouquets of the most beautiful roses
—

To the ones who never experienced it.
To the ones who needed it and didn't know how to ask.
To the ones like me.

Because love is the most powerful act in the universe.
Stronger than any bullet, bomb, or hate.

And in the end...
I became what I needed most.
Love.

That's the essence of my becoming.

 444™: For Better, For Worse, Forever Becoming

Soul Talk:

Little truths to carry in your pocket when the becoming feels heavy:

- That version of you that doubted herself? She got you here.

- Your softness isn't weakness. It's wisdom.

- You are not behind — you are blooming in divine timing.

- Even in confusion, your becoming is working.

- You are not broken — you're breaking through.

444™: For Better, For Worse, Forever Becoming

Safe Space:

Self Reflection

Who am I becoming — and am I allowing myself to meet her with grace?

Self Reflection

What old identities or habits am I ready to release?

Self Reflection

What does healing look like on me today, not yesterday?

Self Reflection

What parts of my journey have I judged instead of honoring?

Self Reflection

What do I need to say "thank you" to — even if it hurt?

 444™: For Better, For Worse, Forever Becoming

Affirmations for Becoming

- I allow myself to grow at my own pace.

- I don't rush my healing. I honor it.

- I release shame about where I've been — I needed those lessons.

- I give myself permission to evolve.

- Becoming me is the most beautiful thing I've ever done.

Love Letters to My Becoming

Dear Becoming Me,

I see you.

Not the polished version, not the final product —

But the messy, magical, half-bloomed woman in progress.

You are the most beautiful thing I've ever grown into.

Thank you for not giving up when you had every reason to.

Thank you for loving me before I even knew how to love myself.

You are becoming, and baby... it's breathtaking.

 444™: For Better, For Worse, Forever Becoming

Dear Little Girl I Used to Be,

They tried to crush your spirit before it could stretch its wings.

But you still whispered to the stars.

Still dreamed.

Still believed there had to be more than pain.

And you were right.

I carried you with me into every battle, and now?

I'm building the life you prayed for.

You are safe here. You are loved here. You are free.

Dear Present Me,

I know you still doubt yourself sometimes.

But look around — look at everything you've created from broken pieces.

You've made purpose out of pain, power out of rejection.

You don't need to rush.

You're allowed to rest.

You're doing it.

You ARE it.

 444™: For Better, For Worse, Forever Becoming

Dear Future Me,

I hope you're still choosing softness,

Still walking in love,

Still giving away roses without regret.

I hope you never forget where you started —

Not to dwell there, but to celebrate how far you've come.

Keep becoming. Keep becoming.

There's no limit to what you can be when you are love.

 444™: For Better, For Worse, Forever Becoming

Chapter Two: Forever Believing

Belief isn't always loud.
Sometimes it's whispering "maybe" while your whole world screams "no."
Sometimes it's waking up with tears still on your pillow,
but still... waking up.
Still breathing.
Still trying.

There were so many moments I could've given up.
So many nights where I laid in silence,
wondering if I mattered to anyone at all.
But every time the smoke cleared — I was still standing.
Shaken? Yes.
Broken? Sometimes.
But standing.

 444™: For Better, For Worse, Forever Becoming

Because deep down, I've always believed
there had to be more for me than pain.
Even when I had no evidence,
even when no one else believed in me,
I chose to believe in myself.

Not because I felt strong —
but because **I had no choice.**

My Story

No matter what I've gone through in life...
when the dust settled and the smoke cleared — I was
always still here.
I didn't have a crowd cheering me on.
I didn't have someone to hold my hand through the storms.
I had **me**.

And so I had to believe in something.
I had to believe in me.

Because if I didn't,
If I didn't hold on to that tiny thread of hope...
I would've been gone a long time ago, sleeping in my grave.

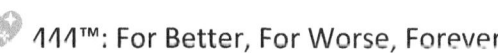

It wasn't pretty. It wasn't perfect.
But every morning that I wake up —
I feel it in my bones, deep down in my soul:
The Creator still has a plan for my life.

And if there's still breath in me,
then there's still purpose on me. (WHEW!!)
READ IT AGAIN!!
And if there's still breath in me,
then there's still purpose on me

And I believe that with everything in me!!
NO EXCEPTIONS!

Soul Talk:

Little truths to hold when your belief feels shaky:

- If I'm still here, I'm still meant to be.

- I was built to outlive every storm sent to destroy me.

- I don't need everyone to believe in me — **I just need to believe in me.**

- My belief is my rebellion.

- The Creator didn't bring me this far to abandon me.

Safe Space:

Self Reflection:

What moments in my life proved that I'm stronger than I thought?

Self Reflection:

What have I overcome that I never thought I could?

Self Reflection:

When was the last time I encouraged myself?

Self Reflection:

What beliefs am I ready to let go of — and what new ones am I ready to embrace?

Self Reflection:

Do I believe I'm worthy of the life I desire? Why or why not?

Affirmations for Believing

- I believe in myself, even when no one else does.

- I trust the timing of my life.

- I am guided, protected, and chosen on purpose.

- I have everything I need inside of me to keep going.

- I was never a mistake. I am the blueprint.

 444™: For Better, For Worse, Forever Becoming

Love Letter to My Belief

Dear Me,

Thank you for holding on when it was easier to let go.

Thank you for choosing to believe in something better —
even when all you had was pain.

You didn't wait for proof. You *were* the proof.

And now... look at you. Look at Us.

Standing. Healing. Growing.

Be proud of the version of you that didn't give up — she's
the reason you're here.

And she still believes.

Always has. Always will.

Forever Believing,

Keesh

 444™: For Better, For Worse, Forever Becoming

Chapter Three: Forever Growing

Growth doesn't always come from healing.
Sometimes it comes from heartbreak.
From betrayal.
From realizing the people you gave everything to —
wouldn't give a fraction of it back.

One of the hardest lessons I've ever learned is this:
You can't expect you from other people.
Not everyone has your heart.
Not everyone loves like you do.
Some people see your kindness as weakness.
Some people prey on it — for sport.

And that hurts more than words can explain.

But here's what I've decided:

I will not let this world harden me.

I was born open-hearted —

and I will grow wider, not colder.

Because even when life breaks me,

I bloom…….HELLO!!!

And every time someone lets me down,

I become more of who I'm meant to be.

My Story

The lesson that still cuts the deepest?
That not everyone has the same heart as I do.
I've had to learn the hard way — painfully —
that my kind of love is rare.
That my level of loyalty, care, and selflessness isn't a
universal language.

And people?
They've taken advantage of that.
Used it. Mocked it. Left me bleeding for daring to love
them in a way they couldn't return.

But the part that hurts the most?
It wasn't just romantic relationships.
It was family.
It was friends.
The ones who should have protected me, uplifted me…
they broke my heart too.

And yet…
with every heartbreak, my heart somehow grew bigger.
With every disappointment, my soul bloomed brighter.

Because I know now:
I was made this way on purpose.
I wasn't created to blend in with cold hearts.
I was designed to remain soft — even in a world that begs me to turn to stone.

Soul Talk

- You can grow through what didn't grow you.

- The pain didn't ruin you — it revealed you.

- Every scar is a sign that you *made it through.*

- There is strength in staying soft.

- You are not too much — you were just too pure for the wrong ones.

Self Reflection:

Who or what helped me grow — even if it hurt?

Self Reflection:

What lesson have I learned that I still resist accepting?

Self Reflection:

Have I allowed painful people to change my heart? Why or why not?

Self Reflection:

What would it look like to grow with boundaries instead of walls?

Self Reflection:

What part of me bloomed after I thought I'd never recover?

Affirmations for Growing

- I grow even in dry seasons.

- I will not let the world make me hard.

- My heart is my gift, not my weakness.

- I choose growth over bitterness.

- Every piece of me is still worthy — even the broken ones.

Love Letter to My Growth

Dear Heart,

I know you've been through a lot.

People have taken from you. Lied to you. Walked away from you like you were nothing.

But you never stopped growing.

You never stopped reaching for light.

And that makes you unstoppable.

Your softness is sacred. Your tears are holy. Your bloom is divine.

Thank you for not giving up on love, even when love gave up on you.

You didn't become bitter — you became *better*.

And that is the most beautiful kind of growth there is.

Still blooming,

Me.

 444™: For Better, For Worse, Forever Becoming

Chapter Four: Forever Chosen

There is a heartbreak that doesn't come from lovers.
It comes from the people who were supposed to love you
first.
The ones who brought you into the world
but somehow forgot to choose you once you were in it.

Being chosen isn't just about someone picking you —
it's about someone protecting you.
Prioritizing you.
Standing in the gap for you when the world goes cold.

But what happens when the people you needed the most
were too busy needing something else?

My Story

My parents' divorce changed everything.
And not just because the family shifted —
but because in the split, **I felt like neither of them chose me.**

Both sides made a decision...
and I was the casualty.
An afterthought in a war I didn't start.
They were both too consumed with their own lives, their own pain —
and when I *was* included, I was never a priority.

So I had to protect myself.
I had to build my own world.

I distanced myself.
Not because I didn't love them,
but because staying close would have drowned me in their feud.
It would've buried me in emotional chaos I didn't cause.

So I became a wanderer.

A survivor.

 444™: For Better, For Worse, Forever Becoming

I trained myself to need nothing from no one.
I absorbed every lesson I could,
learned how to exist in any environment.
Adapt.
Adjust.
Endure.

Each day, I woke up and made it my business to make it to the next day.
And over time, I realized:
If no one was going to choose me,
I would choose myself.

Soul Talk

- Sometimes survival is the greatest form of self-love.

- I didn't get to choose my beginnings — but I *do* get to choose myself now.

- The absence of love taught me how to be the presence of it.

- Choosing me isn't selfish — it's sacred.

- I am not hard to love — they just didn't know how.

444™: For Better, For Worse, Forever Becoming

Safe Space:

Self Reflection:

When was the first time I realized no one was going to save me?

Self Reflection:

How has my survival shaped my independence — and my isolation?

Self Reflection:

Have I truly accepted that I am worthy of being chosen —
not tolerated?

Self Reflection:

What does choosing *me* look like today?

Self Reflection:

What patterns or beliefs am I shedding so I don't abandon myself?

Affirmations for Being Chosen

- I choose me — fully, boldly, and unapologetically.

- I am worthy of care, even when no one else shows up.

- I am not too much. I am just enough for the right people.

- I was never invisible — they just didn't have the vision to see me.

- Being chosen starts with me.

 444™: For Better, For Worse, Forever Becoming

Love Letter to My Chosen Self

Dear Me,

I'm sorry no one stood in the gap for you.

I'm sorry you had to learn how to hold yourself together when all you wanted was to be held.

But I'm so proud of the way you made something sacred out of your survival.

You stopped waiting to be picked —
and you picked *yourself.*

You turned loneliness into loyalty.

You turned rejection into redirection.

And you never stopped believing there was more for you.

You are not forgotten.

You are not second-best.

You are not lost in the shuffle.

You are forever chosen.

And this time — by someone who will *never* leave you again.

With honor,

Keesh

 444™: For Better, For Worse, Forever Becoming

Chapter Five: Forever Healing

Healing isn't soft music and bubble baths.
It's not always gentle.
Sometimes it looks like crying in your car and still clocking into work.
Sometimes it feels like grieving the version of you that never got to live fully.

Healing is messy.
It's lonely.
It's exhausting.
But it's necessary.

Because you can't stay numb and call it peace.
You can't keep abandoning yourself and call it love.
And you can't pretend you're okay when your soul is screaming for help.

Healing is choosing to stop surviving —
and finally start *living*.

 444™: For Better, For Worse, Forever Becoming

My Story

I knew I had to heal when I realized I felt... nothing.

I didn't care about anything.
Not my dreams.
Not my peace.
Not even *me*.

I had gone so numb that I didn't recognize the woman in the mirror anymore.
The fire was gone.
The softness was gone.
Even the pain was gone — and that scared me the most.

I missed the old me.
The one who laughed louder, felt deeper, loved harder.
The person I was *before the world changed me.*

But I realized...
she had to die so I could live.
She was the sacrifice —
and her death would not be in vain.

Because healing for me?
It's not just existing.
It's pushing forward when everything inside wants to collapse.
It's wanting better for myself — even when I've never seen what "better" looks like.

I'm not gullible.
I'm not naive.
I just believe in something more.
And I won't apologize for that.

I want to give my child the things I never had:
A safe home.
Real love.
A thriving environment that doesn't feel like war.

But to give that, I had to confront **me.**

I had to look myself in the face and admit:
"You are 99.5% responsible for the B.S. you've tolerated."

That truth didn't break me —
it broke me *open.*

Now, I follow my heart...
but I take my brain with me.

 444™: For Better, For Worse, Forever Becoming

Soul Talk:

- Healing doesn't mean I'm unhurt — it means I'm *unbreaking*.

- I had to unlearn survival to remember how to live.

- It's not wrong to want better — even if I've never seen it before.

- Some parts of me had to die so the real me could live.

- I am not ashamed of needing time to heal — I'm proud I never gave up.

Safe Space:

Self Reflection:

What part of me went numb — and why did I silence it?

Self Reflection:

Who was I before the world tried to change me?

Self Reflection:

What am I still carrying that isn't mine to hold anymore?

Self Reflection:

What does healing *actually* look like in my day-to-day life?

Self Reflection:

Am I giving myself the love, structure, and softness I never had?

Affirmations for Healing

- I will not shame myself for hurting — healing takes time.

- I deserve a life that feels good to live, not just survive.

- I will not become the pain that tried to shape me.

- Every day I wake up is proof that healing is happening.

- I am allowed to start over as many times as I need to.

Love Letter to My Healing

Dear Healing Me,

I know this journey hasn't been easy.

You've cried yourself to sleep, blamed yourself for things you didn't cause,

and questioned whether peace was even meant for you.

But look at you now.

Awake.

Aware.

Becoming.

You are not weak.

You are not broken.

You are rebuilding — brick by brick, breath by breath.

The old you didn't fail.

She made it far enough to hand you the tools for your next chapter.

She walked so you could finally run.

So run, baby.

Run into your healing.

Run into your peace.

Run into the version of you who refuses to settle for pain ever again.

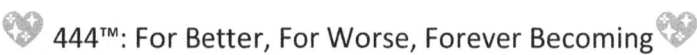 444™: For Better, For Worse, Forever Becoming

Forever healing,
Me.

Chapter Six: Forever Grace

Before I could become the woman I was created to be,
I had to do something most people never talk about…

I had to forgive myself.

Not just the surface things —
but the quiet guilt that lived in my bones.
The shame that stole my voice.
The inner child that still flinched when things got loud.

Grace didn't come easy.
But it came honestly.

And I realized that grace isn't about excusing what
happened —
it's about choosing not to punish yourself for surviving it.

 444™: For Better, For Worse, Forever Becoming

My Story

Before I could walk in purpose,
Before I could write these words,
Before I could even *look myself in the mirror* with love...

I had to forgive me.

I had to forgive myself for staying silent about the abuse
I endured as an adult.
Forgive the little girl inside of me who still thought staying
quiet might keep her alive.

I had to forgive myself for not reacting.
For not knowing how.
For not understanding what was happening — only knowing
that it was *wrong.*

I had to forgive myself for the ripping and shredding of
my own skin...
because no matter how hard I tried, I could never scrub
off the feeling of being violated.

 444™: For Better, For Worse, Forever Becoming

I had to forgive myself for staying in situations that I _knew_ would never love me —
but I just needed to feel _something._

I had to forgive myself for the rage.
For the numbness.
For the destruction every man or woman met when they crossed my broken heart.
I had to forgive myself for wishing death would come find me.

I'm not fully healed.
Not even close.

Some days it still hurts to breathe.
Some nights I still cry for reasons I can't name.
But grace has made room for me to stay.

And the only thing I might never forgive myself for…
is that there were moments where I didn't want to live.
Moments where I didn't believe life could *ever* feel
beautiful again.

But I'm still here.
Grace and grace alone is the ONLY reason.

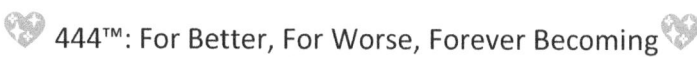 444™: For Better, For Worse, Forever Becoming

Soul Talk

- Grace doesn't erase the past — it reclaims your future.

- **You did the best you could with what you had. That's enough.**

- Healing without grace is just more punishment.

- You don't have to keep bleeding for wounds you didn't create.

- You deserve softness — even from yourself.

 444™: For Better, For Worse, Forever Becoming

Safe Space:

Self Reflection:

What parts of myself have I judged that need grace instead?

Self Reflection:

What have I blamed myself for that wasn't my fault?

Self Reflection:

Where can I show myself more compassion in this season?

Self Reflection:

How would my healing shift if I approached it with grace, not guilt?

Self Reflection:

What does forgiving *me* look like in real time?

Affirmations for Grace

- I give myself grace without conditions.

- I am not my past. I am my perseverance.

- I forgive myself for what I didn't know.

- I am allowed to begin again — as many times as I need.

- Grace is not a weakness. It's my birthright.

 444™: For Better, For Worse, Forever Becoming

Love Letter to My Grace

Dear Graceful Me,

You have carried more than anyone should ever have to.

You've held secrets that weren't yours to keep.

You've carried shame that never belonged to you.

But you made it here — to this moment.

And I am so proud of you.

You didn't just survive.

You softened.

You forgave.

You kept your heart open when it would've been easier to close it forever.

You are not your silence.

You are not your scars.

You are not the worst thing that ever happened to you.

You are *grace in motion.*

And you are finally free.

With love,

Me.

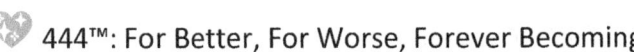 444™: For Better, For Worse, Forever Becoming

Chapter Seven: Forever Love

Love.

It's supposed to be the most beautiful thing in the world.
But for some of us...
it's also the most confusing.

Because what happens when you've *never actually felt it?*
What happens when the only kind of love you've known
came with strings, price tags, punishment, and pain?

I don't know everything about love.
But I do know this:
If it doesn't feel safe — it's not love.
If it makes you shrink, silence, or sell yourself — it's not
love.
If it requires your body, your obedience, your identity,
just to feel seen —
it's not love.

 444™: For Better, For Worse, Forever Becoming

Love doesn't hurt you on purpose.

Love doesn't make you guess.

Love doesn't play dress-up just to disappear when it's inconvenient.

Real love?

It stays.

It holds.

It frees.

And maybe I haven't received it yet...

but I damn sure know what it's *not*.

My Story

Here's the truth:
I don't know what love really feels like.

Not the kind I give.
Not the kind I crave.
Not the kind I've written about in poetry and daydreams.

Of course I'd like to experience it.
But the truth is...
I never have.

The love I've seen and received?
It came with terms.
Conditions.
Price tags.

 444™: For Better, For Worse, Forever Becoming

I had to buy it.

I had to be on my best behavior for it.

I had to give up my voice.

Give up my body.

Sometimes... even sell pieces of my soul.

It was never given freely.

Never offered wholeheartedly.

Never wrapped in *truth*, *protection*, or *grace*.

And now?

If the love someone offers me isn't what I give out —

I don't want it.

Keep it.

Your broken version of love might be all you know,

but it's not good enough for me anymore.

Your breadcrumbs don't fill me.

Your confusion doesn't comfort me.

 444™: For Better, For Worse, Forever Becoming

Love should feel like a warm blanket on a cold morning.
Radiate like sunlight on your skin.
Rock me to sleep like the sea —
not drown me like it.

Love should nurture, not destroy.
Protect, not punish.
Hold, not hurt.

And the only part that breaks my heart more than the love I've missed...
is the love I've never learned to give myself.

444™: For Better, For Worse, Forever Becoming

I still don't know what self-love looks like.
Self-worth? Still working on it.
Some days, it doesn't even feel like a priority —
because my mind is still locked in *survival mode.*
Just get to the next day.
That's the only mission I know.

But I'm not giving up.

Because somewhere, deep down...
I believe that love — real love — starts with me.
And I'm willing to keep trying,
even if I have to learn it one breath at a time.

 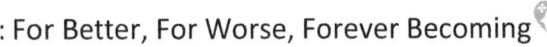 444™: For Better, For Worse, Forever Becoming

Soul Talk:

- Just because I haven't received real love doesn't mean I'm unworthy of it.

- I will no longer accept love that costs me my peace.

- The absence of love taught me exactly what I deserve.

- I am not "too much" — they just weren't enough.

- Real love will never ask me to betray myself.

 444™: For Better, For Worse, Forever Becoming

Safe Space:

Self Reflection:

What versions of "love" have I outgrown — and what am I no longer settling for?

Self Reflection:

Where have I mistaken survival for love?

444™: For Better, For Worse, Forever Becoming

Self Reflection:

What would love look like if it came without conditions, fear, or performance?

 444™: For Better, For Worse, Forever Becoming

Self Reflection:

Can I imagine love starting inside me — and not from others?

Self Reflection:

What is one small way I can love myself better this week?

 444™: For Better, For Worse, Forever Becoming

Affirmations for Love

- I am worthy of love that doesn't hurt.

- I am no longer accepting love that asks me to abandon myself.

- My love is deep, divine, and deserves to be mirrored.

- I am learning to love myself with the same grace I give away.

- Real love will find me — but first, I'm learning to give it to me.

Love Letter to the Love I Deserve

Dear Me,

I know you've been waiting for love to come in like a rescue mission.

Waiting for it to prove that you are worthy.

Waiting for it to fill what the world kept taking from you.

But you're not waiting anymore.

Because now... you know the truth.

Real love doesn't live outside of you —

it starts with you.

You don't have to perform for it.

You don't have to earn it.

You don't have to suffer to feel worthy of it.

 444™: For Better, For Worse, Forever Becoming

Love is your birthright.

And even though the world didn't always show you what it looks like...

you know what it's not.

So keep your softness.

Keep your depth.

Keep your open heart — but protect it this time.

You don't need a fairytale.

You need truth.

And that truth is: **you are already loved.**

You are **forever love.**

– Me

 444™: For Better, For Worse, Forever Becoming

Notes:

 444™: For Better, For Worse, Forever Becoming

Notes:

Made in the USA
Columbia, SC
23 August 2025

61620472R00057